# Prayer For
The Bullies

Kate Pennington

illustrated by Monika Zaper

Published in Australia in 2021 by Kate Pennington

**Website:** www.beyondajoke.org.au

© Kate Pennington 2021

The moral rights of the author are asserted.

All rights reserved.

No part of this publication may be reproduced, stored in a retrieval system or transmitted in any form or by any means without the prior permission of the publisher, nor be otherwise circulated in any form of binding or cover other than that in which it is published.

ISBN 978-0-646-84501-2

 A catalogue record for this book is available from the National Library of Australia

Illustrations by Monika Zaper – **Website**: zaperart.com/monikaz

Layout design by Zena Shapter – **Website**: zenashapter.com

**Disclaimer**
All characters and events in this publication, other than those clearly in the public domain, are fictitious and any resemblance to real persons, living or dead, is purely coincidental.

*For my loved ones: my brother Bruce Pennington, Claire Hodge and Barry Norman Smith, who believed in me always. I honour their memories with all of my love and appreciation for encouraging me to fulfil my dreams.*

# PREFACE

Kate Pennington created Beyond A Joke Incorporated in her brother's memory in order to assist teenagers and young children facing bullying today. Beyond A Joke is creating a domino effect of kindness throughout communities to outweigh the negative effects of aggression and bullying. Kate's ultimate goal and vision is to build safe haven empowerment centres Australia-wide for children and parents to turn to for support and guidance when experiencing any form of bullying.

The philosophy behind the Beyond a Joke book series is to teach children about the values of respect, tolerance, kindness and compassion. Within the series, Kate has used Australian bush animals to teach others about a specific aspect of bullying in a fun, interactive and engaging manner. A workbook section is included at the back of each book to support class discussion about relevant concerns related to bullying, as well as the particular issues identified within each story.

Caron the Cockatiel lived in a lovely rural area of Sydney with beautiful gum trees, wildflowers and lots of other beautiful Australian birds. She was a mother, to a beautiful son named Ashley, whom she loved very much.

Ashley had soft grey and white feathers and a bright yellow head crest. He went to the Birds of Paradise Primary School, where he asked the other birds to call him Ash, as this was the name he preferred.

Ash enjoyed school and made some very good friends. He was popular because he had a very caring personality.

But some of the other birds began to bully him. Conner the Crimson Rosella acted like he was the king of the school and was jealous of Ash's popularity. He got some of the other birds to gang up on Ash as well. Cameron the Black Cockatoo joined in, and so did Gary the Galah.

Ash could not understand why they were being so mean to him. One day, when he opened his lunch box, Conner swooped down from a gum tree and stole one of Ash's favourite worms.

Ash was very hungry and asked Conner to give him back his worm.

Conner just laughed and swallowed the worm meant for Conner's lunch, laughing wildly as he did so.

Ash quickly gobbled up his other two worms before anyone else could take them from him. Ash was very hungry and upset with Conner for snatching part of his lunch away.

Once Ash had eaten the last of his lunch, he turned to Conner and said, 'it is very rude to take someone's lunch. If you want some, you have to ask politely.'

'You have to ask politely,' mimicked Conner.

Gary the Galah and Cameron the Black Cockatoo were sitting on a tree branch behind Conner. They laughed loudly at what Conner had done.

'It's not funny,' cried Ash.

'It's not funny,' they all mimicked in baby voices.

The bell rang and they all flew into the classroom for the last lesson of the day, with their teacher Ms Olive the Owl. Ms Olive was a wonderful teacher and very creative. She was especially good at teaching their home building and improvements class.

'Please sit quietly,' she said to all the birds as they arrived in her classroom, made of vine leaves that twisted around tightly to make a beautiful, sheltered space.

'Today we are going to learn how to make a strong nest in a tree, so that families in their home nests will not be damaged by strong winds. Now I want you all to look at the building materials laid out before you and commence building.'

Ash began to make the most beautiful nest using all the twigs, twine, materials and pieces of wood chips displayed on his desk.

Conner, Gary and Cameron looked over at Ash's beautiful craftsmanship and became very jealous.

'I want to destroy that nest Ash is making,' said Cameron.

'Yes, I do too,' agree both Gary and Conner.

The three of them put their heads together, whispering and planning how they would destroy Ash's beautiful work. They would wait for their teacher Ms Olive the Owl to leave the classroom for more supplies.

'Class, please continue quietly with your work. I am going to gather more straw for those of you who need extra straw for your home nests. I will return in ten minutes, so if you need help before I leave please put up your wing now and ask for help.' None of the birds put up their wings for help so Ms Olive left the classroom to collect more straw.

The three birds looked at each other and quickly flew over to Ash and stole his home nest from him.

'Hey, give that back, it's mine!' cried Ash, helpless with three of them against one.

Conner, who was very unkind, quickly placed the nest in his beak and began to tear it apart.

'Stop!' cried Ash with tears now falling very fast from his eyes.

Conner didn't care how upset Ash was and began to take much delight in how quickly he could destroy the nest. Once completely destroyed, Conner called Ash a cry-baby and went back to his desk with Cameron and Gary.

Ash was so upset he didn't wait for Ms Olive to return to the classroom; he flew home without asking permission to go.

When Ash arrived home, his mother Caron the Cockatiel was preparing dinner. She saw how upset Ash was and stopped everything she was doing to wrap her wings around her son. Gently consoling Ash, Caron asked Ash what had happened and why was he home from school so early.

Ash told his mother all about the teasing, unkindness, stealing and destroying his home nest project.

Caron made Ash a snack and told him he could play with his friend Stan the Sparrow if he wanted.

'I have to go out for a little while Ash so, if you would like to fly over to Stan the Sparrow's tree house to play while I am gone, you can.'

Ash was very pleased with this. He stopped crying and thanked his Mum for being so kind and caring to him.

Stan the Sparrow was a good friend to Ash. Stan had already graduated from school and was on school holidays until university began. Stan was going to gain a degree in Flying Dance. Stan loved to dance high in the sky, gracefully spreading his wings and swooping so low to the Earth then up again into the sky as high as he could go. He was amazing to watch and everyone thought he would be a famous Flying Dancer one day.

When Ash arrived at Stan's tree house and told him everything that had happened at school, Stan offered to cheer Ash up by showing him a new dance routine. Ash was delighted to watch.

Meanwhile Caron the Cockatiel was very upset and angry at what had happened to her son at school. She flew high into the sky, above the clouds, then above more clouds, and then above an aeroplane flying from Sydney to America. Eventually Caron came to the beautiful mystical castle in heaven called God's Kingdom.

God came to the gates to ask Caron why she had come to his Kingdom. 'I need your help please God,' Caron asked hopefully.

'Of course, I will help you,' answered God. 'What kind of help do you need?'

Caron told God everything while God listened to her every word.

'I will send my archangels to speak with these three birds that have turned in to bullies against your son,' he proclaimed.

'Oh, thank you so much, God. I have been so worried flying up to heaven to speak with you about this. I shouldn't have, because of course you have a solution!'

'Go now, Caron the Cockatiel, and relax. I will send the archangels Michael, Uriel and Gabriel to the school to speak with Conner the Crimson Rosella, Garry the Galah and Cameron the Black Cockatoo,' said God.

'Thank you, God,' Caron said again.

God placed his hand on her soft head before she flew back to Earth, assuring her that he was always only a prayer away.

Caron flew back down to the bushland where she lived, feeling so pleased that she had spoken to God about her problem.

When Ash arrived home, she told him what was going to happen and not to worry about the birds anymore.

Ash was happy with his mother and that her love for him was so deep in her heart she wanted to protect him from any bullying.

Suddenly a powerful blue ray of light swarmed into the bush beneath Caron and Ash's home. The blue ray of light then formed into an angel.

Caron and Ash stood in amazement at the sight of God's top angel, the archangel Michael.

'Hello,' Caron said nervously. 'Thank you so much for helping us, Archangel Michael.'

Archangel Michel smiled gently and with love. His blue ray of light symbolised power, strength, courage, protection and faith. He was the perfect angel to help Ash at school. 'I fight for good to win over evil and will empower Ash to gain the courage he needs to overcome his fears and obtain strength to stay safe in bullying situations at school. I am now going to ask Archangel Gabriel to come forward. Are you happy to meet with Archangel Gabriel?' he asked Caron and Ash.

'Yes, Yes, Yes,' they both said immediately.

Archangel Michael then asked Archangel Gabriel to come forward to help him and, as with the appearance of Michael's ray of blue light, a ray of white light shone and then Gabriel stood before them.

Gabriel acknowledged Caron, Ash and Archangel Michael. 'I work closely with children as I am deeply concerned about all children's welfare. I surround you both now with my white ray of light so I can release all the stress and worries affecting you both. Archangel Michael and I will deliver messages to the birds bullying Ash at school.'

'Thank you so much,' said Caron and Ash as they very quickly began to feel the love from both Michael and Gabriel's heavenly energy.

Archangel Michael then said, 'we have one other archangel to bring forward today to help you also.' Archangel Michael then called upon Archangel Uriel to come forward.

A stunning red ray of light entered the beautiful Australian bush. Then standing before them appeared Archangel Uriel.

Uriel acknowledged everyone and spoke directly to Caron and Ash. 'I will bless you with sparks of inspiration, motivation and wisdom whenever you pray to me. I can help you with problem solving and developing confidence to free you from bullying situations that harm and hurt you.'

'Can you empower Ash?' asked Caron. 'I am so worried that when he goes to school he is being bullied and made to cry.'

'Yes, whenever you and Ash pray for my help, I will assist in healing any loss of confidence, and I will help you find empowerment so you both can stand proud and tall, shining with the energy of God's angels. Now Archangel Michael, Archangel Gabriel and I must leave you with the strength from our energy and love while we speak to the birds bullying Ash.'

The three archangels disappeared, leaving behind their rays of colourful light until that too faded into the sky. They arrived at the school and spotted Cameron the Black Cockatoo, Gary the Galah and Conner the Crimson Rosella all sitting together, laughing and smiling as if proud of themselves for making Ash fly home from school crying.

When the three birds saw the colourful blue, white and red rays of light surrounding them, however, they all became very surprised. Appearing before them then were the three archangels.

'What are you doing here?' asked Conner the Crimson Rosella.

Cameron the Black Cockatoo and Gary the Galah sat stunned, so surprised at seeing the three archangels they could not speak.

'We are here to speak with you about your behaviour towards Ash the Cockatiel. Bullying is very unkind,' said Archangel Michael.

'Making another person so upset they cry is very wrong,' added Archangel Gabriel.

'We can help you to understand the importance of kindness and respect towards others, if you wish to receive our help,' said Archangel Uriel.

'Yes, I would like to learn to be kind and compassionate,' said Gary the Galah, in awe of the angel's love.

'Me too,' said Cameron the Black Cockatoo.

'Okay, me too,' said Conner the Crimson Rosella. 'What do we need to do?'

'When you are feeling sad or worried about something, you can simply pray to us for help and guidance, and we can help you. If you start to bully, tease or show unkindness to others, you can again pray to us and we will empower you to be kind and stop bullying.'

'Thank you, archangels,' the three birds spoke. 'Thank you so much for taking the time to empower us to be better birds.'

'I am going to apologise to Ash when he arrives at school tomorrow,' said Gary.

'Yes, I think we all should apologise to Ash,' agreed Cameron.

The archangels now began to leave, knowing they had healed a bullying situation and the sadness of Ash and his mother Caron. The rays of coloured lights from the archangels slowly disappeared.

From that day onwards, Cameron the Black Cockatoo, Conner the Crimson Rosella and Gary the Galah were very kind to Ash and everyone else they met. They had learnt the importance of showing kindness, respect and love to others.

Together now, they would all fly through the Australian trees up high and into the clear blue sky.

Sometimes they would visit Stan the Sparrow to watch his dancing and all the new steps he was learning at university.

Ms Olive the Owl was very happy to see all the birds now getting along well in her class and helping each other with their projects.

Caron the Cockatiel was also happy that she had flown to heaven to speak to God. It was the best thing that she could have done for everyone concerned. The archangels and God had been so kind to answer Caron's pleas for help. They now watched over everyone to make sure that, if anyone needed them again, they were only a whisper in a prayer away.

*Destroying something special that someone else has made is very unkind and can be seen as an act of jealousy.*

*Teasing someone and deliberately destroying their property to upset them and make them cry is bullying.*

*The impacts of this can destroy someone's self-esteem and happiness in life.*

*Be kind always, we all need love and kindness. Having faith in angels, God or whatever you believe in can help you get through difficult times.*

# LET'S CHAT – What are your thoughts?

1. Who was your favourite character in the story?
_____
_____

2. Why was this your favourite character?
_____
_____
_____

3. Who was your least favourite character in the story?
_____
_____

4. Why was this your least favourite character?
_____
_____
_____

5. What would you do if you someone destroying something special another person had made?

_____

_____

_____

6. Would you ever be mean to someone because you thought they were cleverer than you?

_____

_____

_____

7. How do you think you would feel if someone teased you and destroyed your things?

_____

_____

_____

## ABOUT THE AUTHOR

Kate Pennington has worked for many years in long day-care centres, preschools and kindergartens. She has managed before and after-school care centres, as well as a nanny agency. Deciding to further her skills, Kate studied adolescents with behavioural problems. Soon after, she became a foster mother by opening her home to provide emergency accommodation for adolescents.

Kate's aim is to empower people and build them up to be strong, compassionate and caring human beings.

# ACKNOWLEDGEMENTS

I would like to thank all of my friends who believed in me and encouraged me to follow my dreams to help children and teenagers prevent bullying and to show the damage that bullying does to a person's health and happiness.

Many thanks always to Monika Zaper for the beautiful illustrations she produced for all of the characters. No matter what animal or insect I chose for my stories, Monika was able to produce beautiful artwork for each character.

Enormous thanks to Zena Shapter for her creativity and support.

www.ingramcontent.com/pod-product-compliance
Lightning Source LLC
Chambersburg PA
CBHW061135010526
44107CB00068B/2953